# Canada

## For Kids

## People, Places and Cultures

## Children Explore The World Books

BABY PROFESSOR
EDUCATION KIDS

Let's learn some interesting facts about Canada!

In 2012 the population of Canada was around 35 million.

The 2 main languages spoken in Canada are English and French.

Canada is the second largest country in the world by total area .

The maple leaf
is a Canadian
symbol and
features
prominently on
the national flag.

The Canadian motto, A Mari Usque ad Mare, means "From sea to sea."

Canada features the longest coastline in the world, stretching 202080 kilometres (125570 miles).

Canada shares the longest land border in the world with the United States, totaling 8891 kilometres (5525 miles).

Canada is also home to the longest street in the world. Yonge Street in Ontario starts at Lake Ontario, and runs north through Ontario to the Minnesota border, a distance of almost 2000 kilometres.

ge St

Canada has
over 30000
lakes.

Winters can be very cold in Canada with temperatures dropping below -40 °C (-40 °F) in some parts of the country.

Canada's longest river is the McKenzie River in the North West. The river is 2,635miles or 4,241km long.

The highest mountain in Canada is with 19,551ft or 5,959m the Mount Logan in the Yukon Territory at the border with Alaska.

Canada has the largest waterfalls by water volume. These are the Niagara Falls.

Canada is home to about 55,000 different species of insects.

Canada is the second largest oil reserve holder after Saudi Arabia.

Most of the Canadian families have roots in England and France, as during the French and British colonised the country and thus many families from 'the old world' immigrated into Canada.

Inuit are Canada's indigenous people

Canada has a lot to offer and you should visit the country soon and explore!

Visit
BABY PROFESSOR
EDUCATION KIDS
www.BabyProfessorBooks.com
to download Free Baby Professor eBooks
and view our catalog of new and exciting
Children's Books

www.ingramcontent.com/pod-product-compliance
Lightning Source LLC
Chambersburg PA
CBHW080804180726
48003CB00022BA/3002